Got It Goin' On

An Image Awareness Guide for Young "Ladies"

By
JANICE FEREBEE MURPHY

Introduction by
Caryl G. Mussenden, M.D.

&

Message From A Friend
Tuere A. Marshall

Children are surely one of God's greatest gifts and truest challenges. To share your life with a child is to humble yourself so that you may learn from them and discover with them the beautiful secrets that are only uncovered in searching.

—Kathleen Tierney Crilly[1]

GOD grant me the
SERENITY
to accept the things I cannot change
COURAGE
to change the things I can, and
WISDOM
to know the difference

Text: Copyright © 1995 by Janice Ferebee Murphy
Cover: Copyright © 1995 by Janice Ferebee Murphy
All Rights Reserved. No part of this book may be reproduced in any form without written permission from the author.

Library of Congress Catalog Card Number: 96-94048

ISBN: 0-9651166-0-3

Printed in the United States of America
ColorNet Printing & Graphics Inc., Gaithersburg, MD
Fifth printing September 2000

Edited By: Attorney Tara J. Fentress, Children's Advocate

Copyright permission given by:

(1) **EACH DAY A NEW BEGINNING:** DAILY MEDITATIONS FOR WOMEN, copyright 1991, by Hazelden Foundation, Center City, MN. Reprinted by permission.

(2) **NIGHT LIGHT:** A BOOK OF NIGHTTIME MEDITATIONS BY AMY E. DEAN, copyright 1986, by Hazelden Foundation, Center City, MN. Reprinted by permission.

(3) **ACTS OF FAITH:** DAILY MEDITATIONS FOR PEOPLE OF COLOR, COPYRIGHT© 1993 by Iyanla Vanzant
Reprinted by permission Simon & Schuster, Inc.

DEDICATION

First, I would like to thank my Higher Power for all He has allowed me to do and to become. I dedicate this guide to all the women who have played a positive role in my life, especially my mother, and to all those who have believed in me until I was able to believe in myself.

I present this guide out of love and commitment to our children, especially our daughters, who are God's most precious gifts. I also dedicate this workbook to the late Dennis Royce Thomas, a friend, and mentor with The Washington Area Project for Youth, Inc.'s "YOUTH AT RISK" Program. His determination to make a difference in the lives of our youth and inspiration to "be yourself" will forever live in all the lives he has touched.

Speak "LIFE" to our children...for they become what you tell them!

MY GRATITUDE SPEAKS..........

I would like to thank everyone who has been a part of my life; for their belief in me and their endless support.

SPECIAL THANKS TO:

- Family and close friends, especially my Mom & Dad, and sisters, Vallie, Denise and Annette, for their unconditional love, tolerance and patience as I "follow my dreams." Special acknowledgement to my sister-friends Crystal, Donna, Karyn, Lavenia, Pam, Robin, Tara and Tuere for "letting me share" my vision and being my constant cheerleaders. Also, to Warren and the ladies of Argyle Terrace for their encouragement and spiritual support.

- All of the participants in the Washington Area Project for Youth Inc. (WAPY) 1992-93 "Youth At Risk" Program for inspiring this dream.

- Janice Rogers, for her tireless contribution on the computer, her creative layout ideas and her love and patience (and those blueberry breakfast bars and yogurt raisins).

- Attorney Jon Grossman, Dickstein, Shapiro & Morin, L.L.P., for his pro-bono legal advice and friendship.

- The Young Adult Fellowship Ensemble (YAFE) of Metropolitan Baptist Church, Washington, D.C., for their steadfast support and prayers.

- All the young ladies who modeled for the cover: Christy Bates, Kyna Nicole Dunn, Ali Grossman, Natalie Harris, Beni & Anne Hawkins, Claudio Jara-Araujo, Chistine Kaculis, Lisa Lenches, Chiao Liu, Stephanie Martin, Rebekah Phillips, Ragni Rewat, Maria Salinas, Elvia Southerland, Tineal Summers, and Anika & Samantha Williams.

- Shercrisha Finley and Shana L. Ervin, for photographing several of the cover shots.

- Shakenya Harris and the other young ladies who were youth consultants.

- George Valentine II, for his graphic art and desktop publishing expertise, enthusiasm and support.

PREFACE

This easy reading collection of common sense information about self-esteem, peer pressure, developing your natural talents and your personal style, was born out of my struggle to regain my own sense of self after my divorce and other life challenges; and as a result of my mentoring experience with the Washington Area Project for Youth, Inc., "YOUTH AT RISK" Program. I intend for this guide to strengthen the sense of self in some of us, and to ignite a passion for those of us still struggling.

A must have if you are a young woman or have young women in your life!

Peace

Janice Ferebee Murphy

TABLE OF CONTENTS

Message From A Friend i

Introduction ii

Part I: LOVING YOURSELF & OTHERS 1

Self-Esteem & Self-Awareness 3

Respect For Self & Others 12

Values, Decision Making & Role Models 18

Peer Pressure 24

Part II: ENHANCING THE CREATOR'S GIFT - "YOU" 29

Putting Your Best Foot Forward:
Surviving & Succeeding In Today's Society 30

Determining & Developing Individual Strengths
& Talents: Finding Your Gift To The World. 35

Part III: YOUR PERSONAL STYLE 42

Your Personal Fashion Statement 45

Dressing For Success 47

Dressing In Style On A Budget 48

References 51

Research Sources 52

Resources/Services 53

MESSAGE FROM A FRIEND

"When the student is ready, the teacher will appear." I was at a space in my life where I was getting back on my feet, re-entering the world of work, and ready. . . to fulfill the purpose for which God placed me here. At that point God sent into my life an angel, a beautiful spirit, and a genuine best-friend, in the name of Janice Ferebee Murphy. Her gentle, queen-like dignity and grace commanded my respect from our first introduction. Janice's influence and example, and her consistent encouragement and support (she stays on my case), is enabling me to reach goals I set for myself. And when I fall short, we cry and laugh and search for the lesson.

As I grow, I watch Janice grow and realize her goals and aspirations. She is multi-talented and has reached a personal level of success that for many people would be the stopping point. For Janice, however, it is only the beginning. Burning in her heart is a passion and love for our children and the vision of a bright and shining future. She works tirelessly and is always finding new forums to serve "our children".

It is Janice's obedience to that still small voice inside and her discipline that will assure her continued success in realizing her vision for "our children" and fortify her character that I so very much admire, respect and love.

May God continue to bless her and keep her safe for the future of us all.

Tuere A. Marshall

INTRODUCTION

This is a tough time in which to be an adolescent and teenager. There is an inordinate amount of pressure to conform with what's happening in society now, and that does not bode well for young people. Today, there's a pull towards illicit drugs and alcohol, premature and promiscuous sex, violence and instant personal gratification. There's little support to empower our young people to be responsible for their actions and, therefore, their lives. The result of this irresponsibility is drug addiction, recurrent teen pregnancy, sexually transmitted diseases (including AIDS), murder and death and the dependence on the welfare system. *"Got It Goin' On"* is a positive empowerment tool very much needed today.

Empowerment begins with each of us, so I leave you several thoughts:

- *Live your life as an exclamation, not an explanation*
- *Learn to listen*
- *Respect your parents, teachers and others in authority*
- *Pray everyday, not for things, but for wisdom and courage*
- *Read "Got It Goin' On!"*

Finally, dear sisters, I will continually keep you uplifted in my prayers that you will be strong, spirit filled, joyous and successful. I pray that each one of you will grow and mature and leave a great legacy to those who follow you.

My deepest love and respect,

Caryl G. Mussenden, M.D.

PART I:

LOVING YOURSELF

&

OTHERS

*You may not know how to raise your self-esteem, but
you definitely know how to stop lowering it.*
—*Awo Osun Kunle*

Self-esteem is a sense of value and worth that comes from a positive self-image. Self-esteem begins with you and extends to all that you do. With the belief that your best is always good enough, no one but you can destroy your self-esteem. You destroy your esteem when you do not keep your word. When you do not honor the agreements and commitments you make. If you say "yes" when you really mean "no". When you don't follow your first thought. It does not matter what your environment may be. It is of little consequence what your past has been. It is not your concern what others may be saying or doing. It is only in your mind that you build and destroy your self-esteem.

I Am As Great As I Think I Am [3]

SELF - ESTEEM

&

SELF AWARENESS

What do you think about yourself? Do you love/like yourself? In a nutshell, that's self esteem. It's a collection of your thoughts about yourself based on your life experiences and relationships. It can be high, giving you a feeling of value. It can be low, resulting in feelings of worthlessness. Although it takes effort to achieve, high self-esteem is a blessing. This section will explore some steps to help you learn to believe in yourself.

Awareness means knowing what's going on. Self-awareness means knowing what's going on with yourself. Self-evaluation is a reality check into your spirit. It's recognizing your good qualities and your short comings, and accepting the package deal with open arms. This exercise section gives you a chance to look at you. Can you handle it?

From early infancy onward we all incorporate into our lives the message we receive concerning our self-worth, or lack of self-worth, and this sense of value is to be found beneath our actions and feelings as a tangled network of self-perception.
—Christina Baldwin[1]

SELF-ESTEEM: WHAT IS IT & WHAT DOES IT MEAN TO YOU?

SELF-ESTEEM: HOW YOU THINK AND FEEL ABOUT YOURSELF

A. High self-esteem gets you more out of life. Because you feel good about yourself, you:

- Try new things
- Are more productive and effective
- Look forward to doing well
- Get along well with others
- Are accepting of differences in others
- Not threatened by someone else's success
- Feel capable and lovable

☺ Positive self-esteem says:
"I like myself"
"I can do it"
"I matter"

B. Low self-esteem can keep you stuck and hold you back in life. Because you not feel good about yourself, you:

- Are afraid to try new things
- Are less productive and effective
- Feel worthless, incomplete and unlovable
- Tend to be alone a lot
- Criticize or put down others in order to make yourself feel better

☹ Negative self-esteem says:
"I am ugly"
"I can't do anything right"
"Nobody likes me"
"I'll never amount to anything"

C. Your level of self-esteem is determined by a combination of your life experiences and personal relationships in some of the following areas:

- Home
- Social life
- School
- Society at-large
- Workplace

In general, the more positive your experiences and relationships, the higher your self-esteem is going to be. On the other hand, negative experiences and dysfunctional relationships tend to result in lower self-esteem.

D. Building your self-esteem:

Even people with high self-esteem, at times, experience periods in their lives when they don't feel so good about themselves. But that's o.k. It isn't easy to change self-esteem (from low to high), but the rewards are worth the effort. Let's look at ways to improve your self-esteem.

BE YOUR OWN BEST FRIEND

- ♥ Accept yourself for the wonderful person you are

- ♥ Encourage yourself

- ♥ Praise yourself

- ♥ Trust your instincts

- ♥ Love Yourself. Say "I Love You" to you - once a day. And tell someone you love them every day

- ♥ Respect yourself

- ♥ Take pride in your accomplishments

- ♥ Commit yourself to excellence

- ♥ Set realistic short-term and long-term goals

- ♥ Maintain a positive outlook on life

- ♥ Take pride in your individuality

- ♥ Stop watching violent and sexually explicit movies and shows—You become what you see and hear

- ♥ Treat others the way you would like to be treated

- ♥ Develop friendships with girls doing positive things

- ♥ Spend time with people who make you feel good

- ♥ Don't engage in putting other people down. Don't gossip—it does not edify (uplift) yourself or others

- ♥ Volunteer to help others

- ♥ Cultivate a belief in a Positive Higher Power

- ♥ Make a list of your positive qualities and carry them with you. Have someone who loves you help you if you're having a little trouble with this one

- ♥ Accept compliments

- ♥ Do a "Thank You" list

- ♥ Dare to dream, dare to be happy

- ♥ Visualize success

- ♥ Develop plans

- ♥ **GO FOR IT!**

EXERCISE 1

A. SELF ESTEEM:

   1.   HIGH self-esteem: positive statements

        a).

        b).

        c).

   2.   LOW self-esteem: negative statements

        a).

        b).

        c).

   3.   How do you personally demonstrate high self-esteem in your life?

        a).

        b).

        c).

4. What other behavior do you associate with high self-esteem?

   a).

   b).

   c).

5. How do you behave when you don't feel good about yourself (low self-esteem)?

   a).

   b).

   c).

6. What other behavior do you associate with low self esteem?

   a).

   b).

   c).

*It is healthier to see the good points of others than to
analyze our own bad ones.*
—Francoise Sagan

Looking for the good in others is good for one's soul. Self-respect, self-love grows each time we openly acknowledge another's admirable qualities. Comparisons we make of ourselves with others, focusing on how we fail to measure up (another girl is prettier, thinner, more intelligent, has a better sense of humor, attracts people, and on and on) is a common experience. And we come away from the comparison feeling generally inadequate and unloving toward the other girl.

It is a spiritual truth that our love for and praise of others will improve our own self-image. It will rub off on us, so to speak. An improved self-image diminishes whatever bad qualities one has imagined. Praise softens. Criticism hardens. We can become all that we want to become. We can draw the love of others to us as we more willingly offer love and praise. We have an opportunity to help one another as we help ourselves grow in the self-love that is so necessary to the successful living of each day.

I Will See The Good Points In Others Today. And I Will Give Praise.[1]

SELF-AWARENESS: WHAT IS IT & WHAT DOES IT MEAN TO YOU?

SELF-AWARENESS: ABILITY AND WILLINGNESS TO RECOGNIZE BOTH YOUR ASSETS (GOOD POINTS) & LIABILITIES (NOT SO GOOD POINTS)

Knowing and accepting the "good, the bad, and the ugly" about yourself, helps you to recognize what you can play up and what you need to work on. Learning to maximize your assets and minimize your liabilities enables you to become all you can be.

EXERCISE 2

A. LIST YOUR ASSETS AND YOUR LIABILITIES

    1. ASSETS

       a).

       b).

       c).

    2. LIABILITIES

       a).

       b).

       c).

B.   WHAT CAN YOU DO TO PERSONALLY:

   1.   Maximize your ASSETS:

        a).

        b).

        c).

   2.   Minimize your LIABILITIES:

        a).

        b).

        c).

RESPECT FOR SELF

&

OTHERS

R-E-S-P-E-C-T! It's what you give and what you get when you have some of your own. Having a healthy love for yourself allows you to determine, set and maintain behavior that makes you feel good. This enables you to treat others with respect and teaches you to demand respect from others.

Despite the lack of respect for self and others displayed by some young women today, this section offers hope and insight into developing a much sought after and valuable treasure.... R-E-S-P-E-C-T-!

Parents can only give good advice or put them on the right paths,
but the final forming of a person's character lies in their own hands.

—Anne Frank[1]

SELF-RESPECT: WHAT IS IT & WHAT DOES IT MEAN TO YOU?

SELF-RESPECT: LOVING AND CARING ABOUT YOURSELF EMOTIONALLY, PHYSICALLY AND SPIRITUALLY.

You show self respect by taking care of yourself and treating yourself with love. It is also shown by the way you allow others to treat you. You teach people how to treat you by your own behavior. **ACTIONS SPEAK LOUDER THAN WORDS!** Additionally, you show self respect by making decisions that are right for you, as a human being and as a young lady.

A. What does it mean to be a young lady?

    1. How do you demonstrate self-respect in your life in the following areas:

        a). Knowing and respecting your body and demanding that others respect it as well

        b). Boys/sex

        c). Hygiene and grooming

        d). Health and fitness

        e). Body language and speech

    2. How are you able to recognize self-respect in the lives of others?

    3. How can you tell when self respect is lacking?

B. Increasing your self-respect:

As with self-esteem, it's not easy, but the rewards are definitely worth your efforts. Here are some ways to improve your self-respect.

1. Develop a strong sense of self. Spend some time with yourself and get to know what's important to you —what you stand for.

2. Learn to love yourself for who you are.

3. Engage in uplifting activities.

4. Insist on surrounding yourself with positive people: people who speak well of themselves, you, and others.

5. Remove yourself from people and situations that are negative.

6. Stop blaming others. Take responsibility for every aspect of your life.

SISTERCare Code

I will NOT speak badly of another female or allow a female to be spoken of badly in my presence.

I will not ignore when another female is engaged in self-destructive attitudes or behaviors.

I heighten every female's sense of beauty by my love of her.

I do not make fun of, tell lies on, embarrass, or dis-respect another female.

I vow to love myself, respect my body and keep positive thoughts.

What I bring into the life of another female, by the spirit of GOD, will be manifested in my own. (Galatians 6:7)

(Modified from Cecelia Williams Bryant version)

RESPECT FOR OTHERS

RESPECT FOR OTHERS: AS A RESULT OF A LOVE AND BELIEF IN YOURSELF, YOU ARE ABLE TO TREAT OTHERS WITH DECENCY.

> ### THE GOLDEN RULE
>
> ### DO UNTO OTHERS
> ### AS YOU WOULD HAVE THEM
> ### DO UNTO YOU.

A. We all want others to like us, but not everyone is going to like everyone else. It is important that we treat one another with respect.

   List some ways you show respect for others:

   1.

   2.

   3.

   4.

B. "DIS"-respect: What does it mean to be "dissed" or to "dis" someone?

    1.   What are some of the things you have done or have seen others do to "dis" someone?

    2.   How does it make you feel when you "dis" someone?

    3.   How does it feel to be "dissed"?

    4.   Why do you think you do it and why do others engage in this behavior?

VALUES,

DECISION MAKING,

&

ROLE MODELS

Moving ahead with your life takes a lot of courage. There are some key factors that play a major role in this journey. Your values help to determine your behavior. Making decisions allows you to choose the road you will take. Finding people you admire and respect will help you get where you want to go. Where are you headed? Let's take a look.

VALUES: WHAT ARE THEY & HOW DO THEY AFFECT YOUR LIFE?

VALUES: THEY ARE THE BELIEFS PEOPLE CHOOSE TO LIVE BY (THE THINGS THAT ARE IMPORTANT TO YOU). EVERYONE HAS THEIR OWN SET OF VALUES WHICH ARE INFLUENCED BY THEIR OWN ENVIRONMENT.

A. What's important to you? What do you value?

Rank 10 values that are important to you.
(Add to the list and rank in order or importance to you)

Example:	1. Making your own decisions	1
	2. Time alone	5

1. Making your own decisions ____

2. Time alone ____

3. Honesty ____

4. Learning ____

5. ____

6. ____

7. ____

8. ____

9. ____

10. ____

B. How do these people influence your values?

Explain:

1. Classmates (peers)

2. Parents & family members

3. Society (media, church leaders, etc.)

4. Counselors, teachers, coaches, & other school staff

C. How do your values affect your actions concerning:

1. Alcohol & other drugs

2. Violence & other anti-social behavior

3. Sexual relationships & pregnancy

4. Relationship with family & friends

5. Your future

DECISION MAKING

DECISION MAKING: MAKING UP YOUR MIND ABOUT AN ISSUE BASED ON INFORMATION YOU HAVE GATHERED, YOUR PERSONAL EXPERIENCES, YOUR VALUES, AND SOMETIMES WHAT OTHER PEOPLE SAY.

A. Steps to making a good decision:

1. Identify the problem/situation/issue

2. Gather the facts

3. What are your options (be honest and thorough)

4. Look at both the negative and positive consequences

5. Make a choice that you can live with

6. Take action/do something!

Learn to deal with your decision and to evaluate the outcome. This will help you in the future when the situation presents itself again. You may need to do something differently, or you may chose to do the same thing over again.

NOTE: *Values and Decisions made* TODAY = *Determine the Shape of your* TOMORROW.

ROLE MODELS

ROLE MODELS: INDIVIDUALS (PARENT, TEACHER, COACH, ENTERTAINER, ATHLETE, POLITICIAN, ETC.) WHO SERVE AS A MODEL FOR ANOTHER PERSON TO EMULATE (IMITATE). THEY CAN BE POSITIVE OR NEGATIVE.

The emphasis in this guide is on positive influences, but to also address the way in which negative influences can affect your life.

A. Who are your role models and why?

　1.

　2.

　3.

　4.

B. How do these individuals affect your values and decisions?

　1.

　2.

　3.

　4.

C. Do any of your current role models exhibit negative behavior (do drugs, disrespect themselves and others, steal, use profanity, dress suggestively, etc.)? Why do you admire them? Consider removing them from your life and replacing them with positive influences.

D. How does the media influence your choice of role models?

   1. Music videos

   2. Television

   3. Commercials

   4. Magazines

   5. Movies

E. How do you see yourself as a role model? Is it positive or negative? For whom are you a role model and how does it make you feel?

PEER PRESSURE

One of the most difficult parts of growing up is trying to figure out where you fit in. Everyone wants to be liked. Picking positive friends and learning to say "no" to negative people and behavior is not always easy. This section examines some things you can do to handle peer pressure and some of the results of negative choices.

*We need the courage to start and continue what we should do,
and courage to stop what we shouldn't do.*
—*Richard L. Evans*[2]

PEER PRESSURE: WHAT IS IT & HOW DOES IT AFFECT YOUR LIFE

PEER PRESSURE: SUBTLE OR OBVIOUS PRESSURE FROM FRIENDS TO DO THINGS YOU DON'T FEEL GOOD ABOUT.

A. Here are some issues girls (and boys) are often pressured about. Discuss them with your friends and/or an adult you trust.

1. Smoking

2. Drinking and doing other drugs

3. Having sex

4. Hanging out with a particular crowd with a negative reputation

B. How Can I "JUST SAY NO" to peer pressure. The better you feel about yourself, and your values, the easier it becomes to make a decision about being a part of something or not. The greater your sense of self, the easier it is to feel good about yourself even if you're not included.

Tips to help you resist peer pressure:

1. Work on raising your self-esteem. Feeling good about yourself will help you stand up to peer pressure.

2. Get to know yourself. Do things you like and are comfortable with.

3. Be responsible for your own attitude. Let no one choose it for you.

4. Think about ALL the consequences if you go along with the crowd.

    What "HANGIN" could get you:

    ☞ Poor grades

    ☞ Police record/locked up or sent away to a juvenile home

    ☞ Poor health (sexually transmitted diseases, unwanted pregnancies, AID, etc.)

    ☞ Detached from people you love/friends & family

    ☞ **DEATH!!!!**

5. Think about what you want to become and will this activity take you away from that goal. Peer Pressure CAN stop you from doing what you want to do. (JUST ONCE can get you in a *life-time* of trouble! "You better THINK!!!!").

    Here are some things you don't often hear your peers say:

    ★ "Not *everyone* is having sex"

    ★ "Not *everyone* is using drugs"

    ★ "Lots of kids study hard and join school clubs"

Don't Let Girls in the *MINORITY* Blind
You to What The *MAJORITY* Are Doing!

It's wonderful to be popular and special and unique
- but -
you can be "*ALL THAT*" without doing negative things.

When **YOU** are enough, nothing and no one can make you do anything you don't want to do. It's only when you lack self-esteem and self-respect that you feel you must follow the crowd.

BE YOURSELF! HONOR YOURSELF! LOVE YOURSELF!
If you don't, why should anybody else?

P.S. Ask for help if you still feel you can't handle the pressure.

PART II:

ENHANCING THE CREATOR'S GIFT- "YOU"

Do not compare yourself with others, for you are a unique and wonderful creation. Make your own beautiful footprints in the snow.
—*Barbara Kimball*[1]

PUTTING YOUR BEST FOOT FORWARD:

SURVIVING & SUCCEEDING

IN TODAY'S SOCIETY

There are no second chances to make a first impression. Although it may not be fair, society judges you by your outer appearance first, then by what you say (and sometimes how you say it), then by what you do. Learning to love and respect yourself will empower you to take pride in how you present yourself to the world; from health and fitness, to grooming, to the way you dress, walk and talk. This section takes a look at some of the areas young ladies need to pay attention.

PUTTING YOUR BEST FOOT FORWARD

How to make the most of what you already have and "make it" in today's society:

A positive image can put you on the road to success

   A. Getting to know yourself, accepting yourself, and taking care of yourself

      1. HEALTH & FITNESS: A healthy body is the foundation for a healthy mind and high self-esteem.

         a). Develop good exercise habits (physical, mental & spiritual)

         b). Eat a balanced diet

         c). Get enough sleep

         d). Don't smoke, drink, or use other drugs

         e). Get regular check-ups (physical, gynecological, eye, & dental).

      2. GOOD GROOMING: Keep it simple.

         a). Hair: Find a style that fits YOUR face, lifestyle and age

         b). Nails: Keep them neat, manicured and a reasonable length

         c). Feet: Keep them clean and manicured

         d). Make-up (if you wear it): Keep it light, it's only to enhance your natural beauty

         e). Hygiene: **TAKE A BATH OR SHOWER AT LEAST ONCE A DAY, AND BRUSH YOUR TEETH!** ☺

         f). Feminine hygiene: Especially during your menstrual cycle, bathe, change your feminine products regularly and take care of any odor that you become aware of. Sometimes friends are embarrassed to tell you, so be responsible for yourself.

3. **APPEARANCE:**

   a). Dress properly for the occasion. Watch those hemlines and tight dresses. Suggestive dressing can lead to unwanted sexual advances, rape and a poor reputation. Here are a few occasions for you to think about:

   ★ School

   ★ Social function (dance, date, etc.)

   ★ Church

   ★ Sporting events (as a team member)

   ★ Job interview or in the workplace

   (Now you can peak at page 47 ☺)

4. **POISE/ETIQUETTE:**

   a). How you talk (Speak clearly and keep it clean, you're a lady, remember!):

   ★ To your peers

   ★ To adults (parents, teachers, clergy or adults you meet for the first time)

   ★ To younger children

   ★ On a job interview or in the workplace

b).   Manners (make your Momma proud):

   ★   "Please", "Thank you", "Excuse me"

   ★   Saying hello when someone greets you

   ★   "Yes", not "Yeah"

   ★   Letting an elderly or handicapped person have your seat

   ★   Do these sound familiar?

c).   Body Language (the way you "carry" yourself):

The way you:

   ★   Walk: With purpose and direction

   ★   Sit: With respect for yourself

   ★   Stand: Erect and proud

   ★   Use your hands when you speak: With grace and simplicity

The way you present yourselves to society (meaning family, peers and others) **says a lot about who you are and how you feel about yourself. Your self-image can determine a lot about your life.** The more you know yourself and how to present yourself with confidence, the more positive life experiences you will have. On the other hand, limited self-confidence translates to negative life experiences. Give yourself a chance.

Enhance the wonderful qualities that are uniquely yours, rather than focusing on what someone else has. Otherwise, you might miss your own true beauty, and never reach your full potential.

EXERCISE 3

A. How important are first impressions? Describe serveral situations with "good" and "bad" first impressions, including possible results.

    1.

    2.

    3.

    4.

DETERMINING & DEVELOPING INDIVIDUAL STRENGTHS & TALENTS: FINDING YOUR GIFT TO THE WORLD

What makes you so special? It's wonderful when you know what you are good at, and others acknowledge it, encourage and support you. Everyone has a special gift that the world is waiting to experience. Determining and developing those strengths can be exciting and sometimes frustrating. Try to keep an open mind and remember that only one of you was created, and that only you can fulfill your Creator's mission. Here are some tips to tap into your unique qualities.

You cannot be anything if you want to be everything.
—*Solomon Schechter*[2]

DETERMINING & DEVELOPING INDIVIDUAL

STRENGTHS & TALENTS

WHAT MAKES YOU SPECIAL? FINDING *YOUR* GIFT TO THE WORLD WILL GIVE YOU A SENSE OF PURPOSE AND STRENGTHEN YOUR SENSE OF SELF (SELF-ESTEEM).

A. Some ways to determine your natural talents:

   1. Join school and/or church organizations

   2. Volunteer outside of school

   3. Hobbies

   4. Spend time with people you think do interesting things

B. Developing your gifts:

   1. Become active in school clubs

   2. Seek membership in groups outside of school

   3. Attend a school specifically geared toward your interest:

      ★ Duke Ellington School of the Arts

      ★ Fashion Institute of Technology

      ★ Cosmetology school

      ★ Carpentry/electrical/computer, etc.

   4. Find a mentor: someone in the field you're interested in

EXERCISE 4

A. WHAT MAKES YOU UNIQUE?

List some of your special talents:

1.

2.

3.

4.

5.

TO ACHIEVE YOUR DREAMS REMEMBER YOUR ABC's

Avoid negative sources, people, places, things and habits.

Believe in yourself.

Consider things from every angle.

Don't give up and don't give in.

Enjoy life today; yesterday is gone and tomorrow may never come.

Family and friends are hidden treasures. Seek them and enjoy their riches.

Give more than you planned to give.

Hang on to your dreams.

Ignore those who try to discourage you.

Just do it!

Keep on trying. No matter how hard it seems, it will get easier.

Love yourself first and foremost.

Make it happen.

Never lie, cheat or steal. Always strike a fair deal.

Open your eyes and see things as they really are.

Practice makes perfect!

Quitters never win and winners never quit.

Read, study and learn about everything important in your life.

STOP PROCRASTINATING!

Take control of your own destiny.

Understand yourself in order to better understand others.

Visualize it.

Want it more than anything.

X-ray yourself before x-raying others.

You are God's unique creation. Nothing can replace you.

Zero in on your target and go for it.

"LOVE YOURSELF! HONOR YOURSELF! RESPECT YOURSELF!"

PART III:

YOUR PERSONAL STYLE

"True personal style goes way beyond fashion to incorporate such ineffable intangibles as wit, energy, humor, grace of movement, mannerisms, cadence of speech, values, intelligence, heart, and inner sparkle. Your clothes reflect your taste, and even to a degree, what you're about, but they don't change your essence or substance. Great individual style is the perfect blending of a person's essence with the clothes she chooses".[4]

Reared as we were in a youth and beauty oriented society, we measured ourselves by our ornamental value.
—Janet Harris

Rare is the woman who doesn't long for a svelte body, firm breasts, pretty teeth, a smooth complexion. Rare is the woman who feels content, truly satisfied with her total person. We are often torn between wanting to be noticed and yet not wanting eyes to gaze upon us.

We are all that we need to be today, at this moment. And we have an inner beauty, each of us, that is our real blessing in the lives of others. Our inner beauty will shine forth if we invite it to do so. Whatever our outer appearance, it doesn't gently touch or bring relief where suffering is—like our words which come from the heart, the home of our inner beauty.

Perhaps a better mirror for reflecting our true beauty is the presence or absence of friends in our lives. We each have known stunning women who seemed to cast only cold glances our way and handsome men who arrogantly belittled others. It's our inner beauty that is valued by others. The surprise in store for each of us, is in discovering that the glow of our inner beauty transforms our outer appearance too.

My beauty today will be enhanced by my gentle attention to other people sharing my experiences.[1]

YOUR PERSONAL FASHION STATEMENT,

DRESSING FOR SUCCESS,

&

DRESSING IN STYLE ON A BUDGET

As you let your inner light shine (self-love) you will learn how much your clothes say about "you". Because you are a unique creation, let your fashion statement be personal...say something only you can say. You can still be "a part of" with your own way of expressing it; with self-respect. Getting to know what you like, and determining your goals can help you make good decisions about your style, appropriate attire and your fashion budget. This final section brings it all together, a positive self-image and how your personal style can enhance the "NEW YOU". **LOOKING GOOD JUST ISN'T ENOUGH!**

SELF-ESTEEM

If you are not feeling good about you, what you're wearing outside doesn't mean a thing.
—Leontyne Price

YOUR PERSONAL FASHION STATEMENT

PULLING IT ALL TOGETHER

A. How to establish your own personal style:

   1.   Get to know yourself and feel good about yourself (self-awareness)

- ★ Know your likes/dislikes

- ★ Know your body and feel good about it

- ★ Have some lifetime goals in mind

- ★ Know your personality

- ★ Play up your assets: skin, hair, intelligence, voice, etc.

   2.   Study fashion

- ★ What's the difference between:

    a). Fashion trend

    b). Fad

    c). CLASSIC STYLE!!

3. Fashion resources

   ★ Malls

   ★ Movies

   ★ Television

   ★ Magazines
   (Sisters-N-Style, YSB, Sassy, SEVENTEEN Magazine, Essence, Vogue, Ebony, "Right On")

4. Experiment by finding colors and shapes that work for you (clothes, hair and make-up):

   ★ Find "YOUR LOOK" by trading outfits with your girlfriends - make sure they're willing.

   ★ Volunteer to model for a local fashion show. Pay close attention to the clothes - you'll get some valuable fashion tips!

   ★ Bug your older sister or mom (if they've got style!☺) and ask for some pointers.

   ★ Play around with hair, make-up & accessories, keeping in mind the unique style you are trying to create.

DRESSING FOR SUCCESS - "AND WHERE DO YOU THINK YOU'RE GOING IN THAT, MISSY??!!"

WHAT TO WEAR WHERE - DRESSING PROPERLY FOR THE OCCASION

Your clothes say a lot about you. It's not only *what* you wear, but *how* you wear. Make sure your clothes are appropriate for the situation and send the right message. Remember, what's right for you may not be right for someone else, and vice versa. Always be ready to handle the consequences of your fashion choices at:

- School: Check your local malls and current issues of youth magazines for what's in style and appropriate. If you wear a uniform, give some style to your outfit by accessorizing. Remember not to break the school dress code.

- Place of Worship: Always be conservative - dresses and skirts are most appropriate (watch those hemlines!).

- Social functions: Dress according to the function. Have some self-respect - leave the sleezy clothing and wierd hairstyles for those who haven't read *"Got It Goin' On."*

- The mall or just "hangin' out": Same as suggestions for school - be comfortable and tasteful.

- A job interview or in the workplace: Dress for the position you are applying for or the job you are being paid to do. Remember, you want a job, not a date or a part in an X-rated movie!

- Other occasions: Imagine that the FASHION POLICE are standing outside your door each time you go out -

WOULD YOU BE ARRESTED?!

DRESSING IN STYLE ON A BUDGET

How DO you DO that?

A. Where is the money to shop going to come from?

1. Allowance

2. After-school jobs

3. Gifts from relatives

4. Birthdays

5. Other special occasions

4. List other sources

B. Where to get your clothes:

1. Department store sales

2. Designer discount stores

3. Home sewing

4. Second-hand/consignment shops

5. Flea markets

6. Outlet malls

7. Department store clearance centers

8. Catalogs

9. Can you think of other sources

C. When you can't afford all that you want (or anything you want for that matter)

1. Be grateful for what you do have. Learn to want what you have so that one day you can have what you want.

2. Get back in touch with your self-esteem:

    ★ You are lovable even if you can't afford the latest

    ★ You are worthwhile

    ★ The better you feel about yourself, the less needy you will be

3. Be creative:

    ★ Learn to sew

    ★ Learn to bargain hunt (yes you can find what's in style for a lot less)

    ★ Keep it simple

    ★ Get a job

    ★ Swap with friends (make sure they know about it and agree)

BE YOURSELF! HONOR YOURSELF! LOVE YOURSELF!

And most of all, don't take yourself so seriously!

Look to your Creator and within yourself for everything you need.
Thanks for making an investment in yourself
and for supporting my vision.

IT'S UP TO YOU NOW!

and remember .... HAVE SOME FUN TODAY!

REFERENCES

(1) Hazelden Meditations (1982 & 1991). *Each Day A New Beginning: Daily Meditations for Women*. Center City, Minnesota: Hazelden Educational Materials.

(2) Dean, Amy E. (1986). *Night Light: A Book of Nighttime Meditations.* New York: (Hazelden Meditation Series) Harper & Row, Publishers, Inc., arrangement with the Hazelden Foundation

(3) Vanzant, Iyanla (1993). *Acts of Faith: Daily Meditations for People of Color*. New York: A Fireside Book/Published by Simon & Schuster.

(4) Feldon, Leah (1993). *Dress Like A Million (On Considerably Less): A Trend Proof Guide to Real Fashion*. New York: Villard Books, p. 169.

RESEARCH SOURCES

1. Kunjufu, Jawanza. (1984). Developing Positive Self-Images & Discipline in Black Children. Chicago, Illinois: African-American Images.

2. Fornay, Alfred. (1989). Fornay's Guide To Skin Care and Makeup For Women of Color (Covering a Range of 38 Skin Tones). New York: A Fireside Book/ Published by Simon & Schuster.

3. Post, Emily (Revised by Elizabeth L. Post). (1965). Emily Post's - Etiquette. New York: Funk & Wagnalls: A Division of Reader's Digest Books, Inc.

4. Freedman, Rita, Ph.D. (1988). BODYLOVE: Learning to Like Our Looks— and Ourselves - A Practical Guide for Women. New York: Harper & Row Publishers.

5. Pamphlets: District of Columbia Government Department of Human Services Commission of Public Health Alcohol and Drug Services Administration.

6. Black Fashion Museum: An Affiliate of the Harlem Institute of Fashion — 2007 Vermont Avenue, N.W., Washington, D.C.

7. The Young Women's Project: The Purple Pages Social Services Network Guide/1994-1995, 923 F Street, N.W., Washington, D.C.

8. ME & MY FRIENDS! ☀☺☺☺

RESOURCES/SERVICES
General Resources

1. Blue Pages Section of the Yellow Pages
2. Eating Disorder Services
3. Emergency Shelters
4. Ethnic Group Youth Services
5. Social Service Agencies
6. Community Centers
7. Local Police Department/911
8. Mentoring Programs
9. Places of Worship
10. Public/Alternative Schools

HOTLINES !!!! (Use Them)

1. ABORTION - National Abortion Federation Hotline	1-800-772-9100
2. AIDS - National AIDS Hotline	1-800-342-2437
3. AIDS - Teen Hotline/Safe Sex	1-800-234-8336
4. Alcoholics Anonyomous (The General Service Office in N.Y., or your local Yellow Pages)	1-212-870-3400
5. AL-ANON (AL-ATEEN) Family Group, Inc.	1-800-356-9996
6. CHILD ABUSE - Foresters National Child Abuse Hotline Childhelp/ISO, 24 HOURS (Crisis counseling for child abuse & neglect)	1-800-422-4453
7. CRIME VICTIMS ASSISTANCE PROGRAM Hotline	Local Yellow Pages
8. GAY & LESBIAN National Hotline	1-888-843-4564
9. Narcotics Anonymous	Local Yellow Pages
10. PREGNANCY CRISIS Hotline	1-800-492-5530
11. RAPE, ABUSE & INCEST - National Network	1-800-656-4673
12. RUNAWAY - National Runaway Switchboard	1-800-621-4000
13. SUICIDE/DEPRESSION CRISIS Hotline (Referral for other cities) *WORLDWIDE ACCESS	1-202-561-7000

NOTES

NOTES

Got It Goin' On

By Janice Ferebee Murphy

Order Form

☐ Please send me _____ copy(ies) of *Got It Goin' On* at $11.95 each plus $3.00 shipping and handling. Add $1.50 for each additional book. Bulk orders available. Please call for special organization and bulk rates, and shipping arrangements for large orders (over 100 books). Washington, DC residents, please add 5.75% sales tax.

☐ Please send me _____ copy(ies) of *Got It Goin' On*-II at $19.95 each plus $3.00 shipping and handling. Add $1.50 for each additional book. Bulk orders available. Please call for special organization and bulk rates, and shipping arrangements for large orders (over 100 books). Washington, DC residents, please add 5.75% sales tax.

☐ I am not ordering at this time, but please add me to your mailing list.

Name _____

Address _____

City _____ State _____ Zip Code _____

Home Telephone _____

Subtotal _____

Shipping and Handling _____

Total _____

Send check or money order, made payable to:
Got It Goin' On
1221 Massachusetts Ave., NW
Suite 609
Washington, DC 20005-5315
Web Site Address: www.janiceferebee.com
gotitgoinon@hotmail.com

For speaking engagements or comments - (202) 829-2822